The War at Home

The United States
in 1968

by Mary C. Turck

Perfection Learning®

Editorial Director: Susan C. Thies
Editor: Judy Bates
Cover Design: Michelle Glass
Book Design: Mark Hagenberg
Photo Research: Lisa Lorimor

Image Credits:
Associated Press: 31, 35, 46
Maury Englander: 11, 19, 21, 22, 24, 25, 29, 38, 40, 43, 44, 45, 49, 51, 52, 62

Art Today: 28, 36
Library of Congress: 7, 33, 34, 55
National Archives: cover, 4, 10, 14, 15, 16, 17, 27, 30, 56, 58, 59, 60, 65

About the Author

Mary Turck is a freelance writer who lives in Minnesota with her husband, Ron Salzberger, and their two daughters, Molly and Macy. In addition to being an author, Mary has also worked as a teacher and a lawyer.

Printed in the United States of America. For information, contact
Perfection Learning® Corporation, 1000 North Second Avenue,
P.O. Box 500, Logan, Iowa 51546-0500.
Phone: 1-800-831-4190 • Fax: 1-800-543-2745
perfectionlearning.com

Paperback ISBN 0-7891-5840-X

Cover Craft® ISBN 0-7569-0928-7

2

TABLE OF CONTENTS

Prologue 4

Chapter 1
A Light Goes Out 6

Chapter 2
War in Vietnam 13

Chapter 3
Draft and Resistance 20

Chapter 4
Making War on the Protesters 28

Chapter 5
Running for President 34

Chapter 6
Hippies and Yippies 43

Chapter 7
Chicago 48

Chapter 8
The Election 55

Chapter 9
The Darkest Days 59

Sources 65

Glossary 66

Index 71

PROLOGUE

In 1960, Americans elected John F. Kennedy the 35th president of the United States. JFK seemed like a breath of fresh air. He was the youngest man ever elected. His friendly grin drew cheering crowds. People looked forward to the "New Frontier" that he promised.

Reporters flocked around his wife, Jackie, who was beautiful and charming. The Kennedy children, Caroline and John, became instant celebrities. Photographers snapped pictures of Caroline riding her pony. They photographed the children playing in the president's office.

Movie stars, authors, and musicians came to the White House. The presidency defined **glitz** and glamour.

John F. Kennedy

In his **inaugural** address, JFK challenged Americans. He said, "Ask not what your country can do for you—ask what you can do for your country." For years, the government had helped people climb out of the **depression**. It was now time for the people to help themselves and others.

JFK started the Peace Corps, sending volunteers to help poor nations throughout the world. Thousands of Americans volunteered.

Other Americans worked for justice at home. They joined the **Civil Rights** movement. They worked toward ending **discrimination** against black Americans.

Then in 1963, JFK was shot and killed. Televisions across the world showed his **grieving** wife and children. The **assassination** shook the nation and the world. Had the new era ended?

John F. Kennedy was killed while riding in a motorcade through downtown Dallas on November 22, 1963. The accused gunman was Lee Harvey Oswald.

Before he could be tried for the assassination, Oswald was killed by Jack Ruby in the basement of the Dallas Police Department.

Vice President Lyndon Baines Johnson became president. LBJ promised to continue Kennedy's work. He tried to keep the dreams alive.

LBJ supported the Civil Rights movement. He declared a War on Poverty in the United States. He promised to make this country a "Great Society."

In 1964, LBJ ran for president. He won by a huge majority. Voters shared his dream of a Great Society.

By 1968, the dream had turned to a nightmare. Anger and despair replaced hope. Crowds of protestors filled the streets. What had happened to the dream?

CHAPTER 1

A Light Goes Out

LEFT OUT OF AMERICA

Cabrini Green was a government-built housing project in Chicago. Tens of thousands of people lived there. They crowded into tall apartment buildings and **row houses**. Most of the residents were black.

In 1968, Cora and her six-year-old son lived in Cabrini Green. At the time, they were friends of the author. They lived on the 11th floor of a high-rise building. The elevators were often broken, so Cora and her son had to walk up 11 flights of stairs.

In front of Cora's building was a parking lot. Sometimes people sold drugs there. A tiny playground stood next to the lot. The playground, like the parking lot, was covered with blacktop. Broken bottles often littered both. Cora did not let her son go to the playground. He had to stay in the house all day.

Cora's son was in first grade. Jenner School was less than a block away. Cora walked her son to school every day, and a neighbor walked him home. Cora was afraid of street gangs, and she was determined to protect her son.

Jenner's classrooms were crowded, and its teachers were overwhelmed. The first-grade teacher looked at the quiet little boy

Crowded tenement housing

and decided that he was **retarded**. She wanted to send him to a special class for slow learners.

Cora refused. She had a **tutor** from the church work with her son. Soon the boy was able to show the teacher that she was wrong. He was not retarded.

A few years later, he would transfer to a school for gifted children. But in 1968, that was still in the future.

Cora loved her son. She helped her neighbors. She kept her home neat and clean. She took the bus to work every day.

In 1968, television showed images of American family life. In these pictures, parents and children lived in single-family homes. Bright green lawns stretched to quiet streets. Dad went off to work every day, wearing a suit and tie. Mom stayed home and took care of the children and the house. Children rode bicycles and played with dogs.

Almost every TV family was white. Almost every TV commercial showed white people.

Cabrini Green did not look like TV America. Its streets were crowded, dirty, and noisy. Black families lived in crowded apartments. Most children did not live with both parents. No one had lawns or dogs. People in Cabrini Green felt left out of America.

In 1967, black people had rioted in 27 United States cities. They wanted the "TV life." President Johnson appointed the Kerner Commission. He ordered the commission to report on the riots.

Kerner Commission

In August 1967, President Lyndon B. Johnson ordered a Commission on Civil Disorders. He appointed Governor Otto Kerner of Illinois as its chairperson. This commission later became known as the Kerner Commission.

On March 1, 1968, the commission issued its report on racial conditions in America. The committee had found that most rioters were young men between 15 and 25 years old. They were school dropouts who had never lived anywhere but in the ghettos. And they were full of hatred toward the middle class—black and white. These young men did not trust the political system or the police.

Black neighborhoods had crime rates 35 times higher than most white neighborhoods. Without many health centers, infant-death rates were high. Trash built up because of poor trash collection standards, so rat bites were frequent. Because they couldn't afford to live anywhere else, more and more blacks moved into the already crowded **ghettos**. Living conditions became unbearable.

The commission's list of horrible conditions went on and on.

The commission report made the following conclusion. "Our nation is moving toward two societies, one black, one white—separate and unequal." The report said the country was still segregated. It pointed to black ghettos in the cities. Black ghettos suffered from poverty. People in them suffered "a destructive environment totally unknown to most white Americans."

APRIL 4—ASSASSINATION

Dr. Martin Luther King Jr. led the Civil Rights movement in the 1950s and 1960s. He preached **peaceful resistance** to overcome evil. He asked people to love their enemies.

Dr. King had a dream that one day "little black boys and black girls will be able to join hands with little white boys and white girls as sisters and brothers."

As 1968 began, Dr. King must have been tired. He had worked hard, traveling from state to state. He had marched and given speeches. He was planning a Poor People's **March** on Washington, D.C.

In late March, the Memphis garbage workers asked Dr. King for help. Most of the garbage workers were black. For a lifetime, they had lived with **disrespect**.

These workers were trying to organize a **union**, but the city refused to **negotiate** with them. The workers went on **strike**.

Dr. King went to Memphis on March 20. He talked with the workers. But he had to leave because of other **commitments**.

Dr. King returned on March 28 to lead a march. The march ended in violence. Dr. King was horrified. He had preached peace, not violence.

Dr. King had to leave again, but he returned in April. On Wednesday night, April 3, he spoke at the Masonic Temple. During his speech, he talked about threats on his life. And he

Dr. Martin Luther King Jr.

talked about the difficult days ahead. But he encouraged his listeners with the promise of better times to come.

That night, Dr. King stayed up late. He talked and joked with his brother and friends. The next morning, he slept late. After he awoke, he worked on plans for the next march of the garbage workers.

Dr. King dressed to go out for dinner. He stepped out on the balcony of his motel room. He joked with friends down in the courtyard. Then a shot rang out. Dr. King fell bleeding to the floor and died.

James Earl Ray confessed to killing Dr. Martin Luther King Jr. Three days after confessing, Ray filed a **petition** stating that he did not commit murder. He was denied a trial and sentenced to 99 years in prison. Ray died in 1998 still proclaiming his innocence.

DEATH OF A DREAM

For many people, Dr. King stood for the Civil Rights movement. He stood for justice and equality. He stood for that dream. And now he was dead.

Many black people saw hope in Dr. King and the Civil Rights movement. They believed their children would have a better future. But Dr. King was killed, and for many people, hope died with him.

Across the country, cities exploded in anger—Memphis, Manhattan, Boston, Detroit, Durham, Jackson. Smoke from fires set by rioters rose above Washington, D.C. In Chicago, looters robbed stores. Then they set the stores on fire. In Tallahassee, Memphis, and Minneapolis, people were killed.

Cabrini Green exploded too. Teens roamed the streets. People looted nearby stores. Some set fires.

Riots flared, **subsided**, and broke out again. Before it was over, riots hit 130 cities. Riot troops and **National Guard** members patrolled city streets. Mayors set **curfews**. Finally, quiet was restored.

By the time the riots ended, some 20,000 people had been arrested. Thirty-nine people had been killed. Thirty-four of them were black.

A young girl is arrested in New York City.

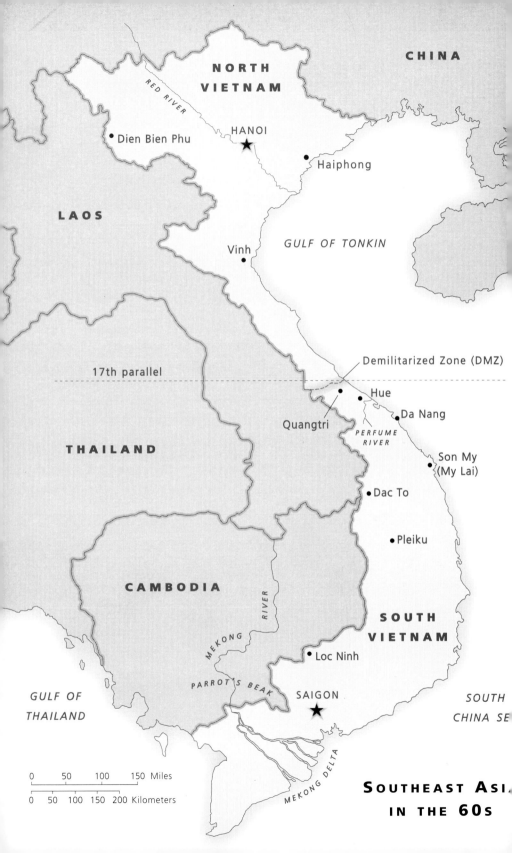

War in Vietnam

While riots seemed like war in the cities, another war raged across the Pacific in Vietnam. Americans fought in both wars.

HOW IT BEGAN—VIETNAM

Like the United States had done two centuries earlier, Vietnam was fighting a war for freedom. Just as England had once ruled the United States, France ruled Vietnam. For ten years, the Viet Minh army fought for freedom from France. In 1954, Vietnam won its independence.

The Viet Minh was the League for the Independence of Vietnam. It was made up of **Communist** and nationalist groups that led the Vietnamese struggle against French rule.

French and Vietnamese leaders went to Geneva. They made a peace **treaty**, which divided Vietnam into two parts. The 17th **parallel** was the dividing line.

The Viet Minh and their allies would move north of the line. The French and their allies would move south.

Ho Chi Minh

Over the next two years, the French would withdraw gradually. By 1956, the whole country would **reunite**. Then all of Vietnam would elect its new government.

In the United States during the Revolutionary War, General George Washington led America to independence. He then became the first president.

In Vietnam, Ho Chi Minh had led the Viet Minh to independence. He became the first president in North Vietnam.

But Ho Chi Minh was also a Communist. The United States feared Communists. Communists believed everyone should share the wealth of the country. They felt no one should be rich. The government should own big businesses. All the money should be shared equally by the people.

In Russia, Communists took over the country after a revolution in 1917. The revolutionists threw out the **czar** and took over the government. The Russian Communists became **dictators**. They jailed or killed people who disagreed with them. They did not allow people to have opinions other than those of the Communist government.

Communists had political parties in many countries. Many people thought all Communists were like those in Russia. The United States government agreed.

The United States had backed France during the war. Now it backed the southern leader, Ngo Dinh Diem.

Ngo Dinh Diem was a **corrupt** ruler. He put his family and friends in top government jobs. His friends and family got government contracts. Often they didn't do the jobs, but they were paid anyway. They were robbing the country.

Ngo Dinh Diem was a bad ruler, but he was an anticommunist. That was enough for the United States.

In 1956, it was time for Vietnam to reunite. It was time for elections.

Ho Chi Minh was ready. He was a popular leader. He would surely win the election.

In the south, Ngo Dinh Diem refused to allow elections. He would not allow Ho Chi Minh to win. The United States continued to back Ngo Dinh Diem.

THE UNITED STATES GOES TO WAR

Ho Chi Minh wanted to reunite Vietnam. He led the Viet Minh back into war. They had won independence from France. Now they would fight for unity.

The United States sent military aid to Ngo Dinh Diem. Dwight Eisenhower was the United States president. He sent United States military advisers to Vietnam. These "advisors" were United States soldiers who were to help keep peace.

Marine helicopter delivering military aid to South Vietnam

Soldiers in Vietnam

In 1961, John F. Kennedy became president. JFK continued to support Ngo Dinh Diem. By the end of 1962, more than 11,000 United States military "advisers" were in Vietnam.

Finally, South Vietnam's army rebelled against Ngo Dinh Diem. On November 1, 1963, the army overthrew Ngo Dinh Diem and took over the government. Now military leaders ruled the country.

After President Kennedy was assassinated, Lyndon B. Johnson became president. He continued to support South Vietnam.

> If this little nation goes down the drain and can't maintain her independence, ask yourself, what's going to happen to all the other little nations?

LBJ sent more and more soldiers to Vietnam. Soon United States troops fought alongside the South Vietnamese. United States planes bombed the countryside.

Anyone who opposed the South Vietnamese government was an enemy. Some fighters came from the North. They were the North Vietnamese Army (NVA). Many others came from the South. They were the National Liberation Front, or Viet Cong. But all fought against the government of South Vietnam.

The Viet Cong did not fight like an army. They were **guerrilla** fighters who had the support of the NVA. They did not wear uniforms nor did they march and salute. They just fought.

Many Viet Cong were part-time fighters. They tended their farms and held regular jobs. But as soldiers, they buried land mines, carried guns, or just fed their fellow fighters. They fought against South Vietnam's government. More and more, they fought against the United States military.

Captain Edward Banks served in Vietnam. Later, he described the guerrilla war.

> It's not like the San Francisco 49ers on one side of the field and the Cincinnati Bengals on the other. It's just not like that....the enemy [was] all around you. One second you may be fired upon from the rear, the next second from straight ahead, or either **flank**. You never [knew].
>
> In other words, you never knew who was the enemy and who was a friend. They all dressed alike. They were all Vietnamese. Some of them were [Viet Cong], but they all looked alike.

United States soldier in Vietnam

HEY, HEY, LBJ

Many United States citizens opposed the war. They had different reasons for antiwar feelings.

Some believed the United States had no business fighting in Vietnam. They asked why the United States should go to war in Asia? Why should the United States support dictators? They felt the United States had too many poor people at home. United States money should be spent on Americans, not on a **foreign** war.

Other people believed the United States was on the wrong side in Vietnam. They felt the South Vietnamese government was bad. It did not have the support of its own people. Those on top stole from the country.

These Americans felt Ho Chi Minh was a better leader. He might be a Communist, but the Vietnamese liked him. And the Vietnamese were the ones who had to live under his rule.

Some people were pacifists. Pacifists opposed all war and violence.

Protesters marched, sang, and chanted. "All we are saying," they sang, "is give peace a chance."

LBJ defended the war by sending more and more soldiers. By 1968, more than 500,000 United States soldiers were in Vietnam. United States planes dropped bombs on farms and villages.

Back home, protesters chanted, "Hey, hey, LBJ. How many kids did you kill today?"

PROTEST GROWS

Young people joined political movements. Many began by working for the Civil Rights movement. Some left college campuses to work for equal rights. High school and even grade school students joined in.

The antiwar movement grew. Many parents and grandparents joined.

In 1967, Dr. Martin Luther King had spoken out against the war. He opposed the war for two reasons. First, he said, violence was wrong. Second, the war took money away from the poor.

The United States spent a lot of money on war. It cost about $322,000 to kill each enemy soldier. That money could help poor people. Only about $53 went to help each poor person in the United States. In one speech, King preached that the peace movement should join forces with the Civil Rights movement.

King's statement angered many. They said the war was not his business. They felt he should stick to civil rights.

Young protesters disagreed. They saw a connection between war in Vietnam and injustice at home. Both war and injustice came from the same political system. That system, said the protesters, had to go.

Dr. King proposed a revolution of values instead of a world revolution. He felt that the United States needed to focus on its own people.

3

CHAPTER

Draft and Resistance

DRAFTING AN ARMY

The United States needed soldiers. The government used the military **draft** to get them.

In the 1960s, the draft law ordered every young man to register. A boy's eighteenth birthday was his personal registration day. After that, he could be drafted.

The draft law provided for some **deferments**. Someone with a deferment would not be drafted.

DEFERMENT—HOME FREE

The draft law set up deferments for medical reasons, for conscientious objectors, for religious workers, and for students.

A medical deferment meant that the draftee was not **fit** for the army. Medical deferments included everything from mental illness to a missing leg. If a doctor said the draftee was not fit to serve, he would get a medical deferment. That seemed fair, but often it was not.

Long after the war ended, James Fallows told a television interviewer about his memories of that time.

Buses started arriving from a white working-class district of Boston. And while nine out of ten of my **comrades** from Harvard and MIT were getting out [of the draft] with their doctors' excuses, the same proportion of people from this part of town were marching right through, going off to the military, going off to the war. Nobody could avoid recognizing what that meant then. We knew that while we were not going to war, we were seeing the people who … were going to be killed.

The law also gave deferments to conscientious objectors, or COs. Under the law, conscientious objectors had to object to all wars. Their objections had to be based on religious beliefs.

Pacifists opposed all war and violence. They believed any war was wrong. But since these beliefs were not based on their religion, they usually didn't receive a deferment.

Some people opposed only the Vietnam War. They believed that World War II was a **just** war. They believed the Vietnam War was unjust. They did not get deferments as conscientious objectors.

Local draft boards decided who received deferments. Some board members did not like conscientious objectors. They felt the objectors were avoiding their duty to their country. That board would refuse CO deferments.

Religious workers got deferments too. If someone was a priest, minister, or rabbi, he would not be drafted.

At first, students got deferments. If a young man could pay for college, he could escape the draft. After graduating, the student could go to graduate school and still keep his deferment.

Poor people could not afford to go to college. So they were drafted. More black men were poor, so more blacks were drafted. Stokely Carmichael attacked the war in a 1967 protest speech.

> When [politicians] get up on television, and Lyndon Baines Johnson talks all that garbage about he's sending boys over there to fight for the rights of colored people, you ought to know that's a lie. 'Cause we live here with [white government officials], and they don't ever do a thing for us.

Carmichael urged black men to refuse the draft.

> We're asking Negroes not to go to Vietnam and fight but to stay in Greenwood [Mississippi] and fight here. We need Black Power.

Stokely Carmichael

Stokely Carmichael was a young black **activist** during the 1960s. In 1964, Carmichael graduated from Howard University and joined the Student Nonviolent Coordinating Committee (SNCC). In 1966, he was elected the chairperson of the SNCC.

Even though he promoted nonviolent activities, Carmichael became more and more discouraged by the results. He coined the phrase "Black Power." Many, including Dr. Martin Luther King and Roy Wilkins, head of the National Association for the Advancement of Colored People (NAACP), felt Black Power urged blacks to unite and end segregation by any means possible—even violence.

JUST SAYING NO

Many protests focused on the draft. Some young men refused to be drafted. Some believed that the war was wrong. Others did not want to die in Vietnam. Or they did not want to kill Vietnamese people. Their words of protest echoed across the nation.

David Harris organized against the draft. He worked to get young men to return their draft cards to the government. In a 1967 speech, he said

> This is a very simple, open, public **declaration** that we will not cooperate, and if the government intends to enforce the Selective Service Act, then it is going to have to send us to jail.

Harris wanted white college students to risk their own futures. He said they had to "put up or shut up." He told them

> Stop screaming against the war and then coming home and making sure you have your student deferment in your pocket. If you are going to be against the war, then put your body where your mouth is.

Thousands followed his example. Some, including Harris himself, served jail time for their acts.

Other young men decided to resist in quieter ways. Some left the country to avoid the draft. Others tried to get medical deferments. They pretended to be lame, crazy, or sick. They tried to fool the draft board or doctors.

SOLDIERS AGAINST THE WAR

Some soldiers **deserted**. They ran away from the war. If they were caught, they were **court-martialed**. Then they were sent to a military prison. Those who weren't caught had to find **refuge** in a foreign country or risk arrest if they returned to the United States

Some soldiers refused to fight. A French newspaper reported that 109 soldiers in a single division refused to fight.

Some returning soldiers formed the Vietnam **Veterans** Against the War. They joined antiwar protests. Many sent their medals back to the White House.

Medals are awarded to soldiers for various reasons. The most important is the Medal of Honor that is given for **gallantry** in action. Other medals include the Distinguished Service Cross, the Silver Star, the Bronze Star, and the Purple Heart.

PROTEST BUILDS

Protesters found many ways to oppose the war. They staged teach-ins on college campuses. Students gathered in auditoriums and listened to speakers protest the war.

Some protesters held **vigils**. They stood silently outside draft boards or government offices. The big signs they held told why they were there.

And always the protestors marched. They marched to Washington, D.C. They marched around the Pentagon. They marched in every large city and on almost every college campus.

The marchers protested the war and the injustice at home. They demanded equal treatment for black Americans and food and housing for the poor. They demanded justice and a new society.

Men burning their draft cards

Antiwar protests grew. In October of 1967, hundreds of young men burned their draft cards.

In Oakland, protesters surrounded a military draft center. Police beat some and arrested others. The next day, more than 10,000 marchers returned. They blocked streets and stopped buses full of draftees.

In November, tens of thousands marched on the Pentagon. Some put flowers in the gun barrels of soldiers. Others cursed the soldiers and called them dirty names. As night fell, police cleared the crowd. Some demonstrators were injured.

BURNING ISSUES

In 1968, four protesters went to draft board offices in Catonsville, Maryland. One was a priest, Philip Berrigan. He was a World War II military veteran. He and the others believed in nonviolent means of protest.

The four men broke into the offices and poured blood on draft records. They were arrested, tried, and sentenced to prison.

Before they went to prison, Philip Berrigan and eight other people went to another draft board. This time, they took the records and set them on fire.

Daniel Berrigan was one of the eight. He was Philip's brother and also a priest.

Brothers Philip and Daniel Berrigan headed the FBI's most wanted list for a while. They were sentenced to three years in prison for their actions at the draft boards. They went into hiding until they were caught and jailed several years later.

Philip has been arrested more than 60 times during peace protests and has spent about nine years in jail. In 2000 at the age of 76, he was convicted of illegally entering a National Guard base and damaging two $8-million jet fighters as a protest to nuclear war.

Despite their protests, the brothers were nominated for the Nobel Peace Prize in 1997. They founded and still run Jonah House, a community committed to a nonviolent approach to fighting the arms race.

Some protesters even burned American flags. They saw evil in America. They saw racism and poverty at home. They saw an unjust war in Vietnam. They saw the flag as a symbol of war, **racism**, and hatred. They burned the flag to reject America.

Flag-burning protests enraged many Americans. They said that burning the flag was wrong. It was an attack on America. Protesters were arrested and jailed for destroying the flag.

In April 1969, the Supreme Court ruled that flag burning was a form of free speech. The First Amendment protects free speech. Surprisingly, some veterans agreed.

Combat veteran Mike Smith agreed with the Court. He was

quoted in a Web site dedicated to free speech. He said that while he disagreed with burning the flag, he supported freedom of choice. He said that he served in the military to protect that freedom.

Quoted on the same Web site, Ivan Warner, a soldier who was taken prisoner by the North Vietnamese during the war, agreed. He explained his thoughts in a quote about being interrogated by the enemy. He was shown a photo of a protester and told that the people of his country did not support his cause. He disagreed. His cause was freedom. And people in his country supported freedom—even when that meant disagreeing.

Soldiers raising the American flag

CHAPTER 4

Making War on the Protesters

Patriots are people who love their country. American patriots believe that the United States is the greatest country in the world. In 1968, many patriots feared Communism. They thought Communists wanted to destroy the United States.

By 1968, most Americans wanted the United States soldiers out of Vietnam. But that did not mean they approved of the protesters. Many people thought protesters were unpatriotic. They said protesters did not love America. They feared that protesters were communists.

WHAT KIND OF PROTEST?

Many Americans feared protest. They thought protesting the war weakened the country.

Domestic policy is the term for what the government does at home. The War on Poverty was a domestic policy. So were civil rights laws. These policies touch people inside the United States.

Foreign policy is the term for one government's actions toward other countries. Foreign policy affects relationships between countries. The United States' involvement in Vietnam was part of our foreign policy.

Protests against domestic policy seemed like family arguments. They were acceptable. But protests about foreign policy were different. Those protests seemed like taking sides against one's own country. They were very unpatriotic.

AMERICA: LOVE IT OR LEAVE IT

Families and friends of soldiers worried about their loved ones fighting in Vietnam. They didn't agree with the protesters.

One construction worker expressed these feelings.

> I got a family. My boy went into the army when he was 18 years old and a day. Suppose they come over and take over the country. What are you going to do then if you don't back up your own president? And I don't care who's president, we back him up. And that's what all the working men do. They love the flag of this country. And they live here. And they're going to do everything they can to protect it.

Sometimes protesters called soldiers "baby killers." Many protesters thought soldiers did horrible things in the war. The name-calling made the soldiers' parents angry. They wanted to strike back.

Vietnam War supporters

Angry people sometimes attacked protesters. So did police. "This is our country," people screamed. "If you don't like it, get out!" Cars sprouted bumper stickers that said "America: Love It or Leave It."

GOVERNMENT WAR ON PROTESTERS

In 1967, Senator John Stennis stated that the protesters were led by communists. He felt those who demonstrated were "cooperating with and assisting our enemy."

Government officials feared protesters and tried to stop them. They ended up waging war on protesters. One of their weapons was the FBI. The FBI, or Federal Bureau of Investigation, is a federal law enforcement agency.

Before the Vietnam War protest began, the FBI targeted civil rights groups. In the 1960s, the FBI set up COINTELPRO, the **Counterintelligence** Program. One of its targets was the Black Panther Party.

During the 1960s and 1970s, the FBI director J. Edgar Hoover set up COINTELPRO to identify, disrupt, and destroy **progressive** community organizations formed by American citizens. Some targets included Martin Luther King's Southern Christian Leadership Conference, free health clinics, and women's groups.

Activities of the COINTELPRO agents included illegal wiretaps, paying informants to join community groups, inciting peaceful groups to violence, giving out wrong and damaging information about groups, and committing criminal acts of violence.

J. Edgar Hoover

Bobby Seale addresses listeners during a Black Panther rally.

BLACK PANTHERS

The Black Panthers scared the FBI. They scared a lot of people.

The Black Panther Party for Self-Defense was founded in 1966 by Huey P. Newton and Bobby Seale. A chief goal of the group was to protect the black community from police **brutality**.

Unlike Dr. King, the Black Panthers said they would use violence to defend themselves. Panthers carried guns for "self-defense."

They called police *the enemies of black people*. Their newspaper called police *pigs*. In turn, the police attacked Panthers.

But violence was not the only Panther focus. The Black Panthers organized in black communities. They ran free breakfast programs and free health clinics. They tutored black children. The Panthers worked to build black pride.

Sometimes COINTELPRO spies pretended to be Panthers to destroy the group from within. Other times COINTELPRO tried to get other groups mad at the Black Panthers. For example, COINTELPRO sent an anonymous letter to a gang leader in Chicago. The letter said the Panthers were going to kill him. They wanted the gang to attack the Panthers.

The FBI and COINTELPRO worked with local police. Sometimes the Panthers fought back when police raided their homes. At other times, they did not.

On December 4, 1969, police raided a Chicago apartment. Black Panther leader Fred Hampton was sleeping. Police forcibly entered the apartment and shot Hampton. He died at the scene.

Fred Hampton was 20 years old and a leader for the Chicago chapter of the Black Panther Party. Hampton was a powerful speaker with skills to organize people. The FBI saw him as a threat to the white population. The FBI and the Chicago police said they stormed the apartment searching for weapons and were fired on by the Panthers. After killing Hampton, the police felt they had done the right thing. They had removed a dangerous criminal from the streets.

The Black Panthers, however, felt that Hampton hadn't had a chance to fight back. They said that the police entered the apartment with guns blazing. Hampton had been murdered by order of the FBI.

Today, the Freedom of Information Act provides that any person has the right to request Federal documents and other information. Therefore, the general public has become more aware of the illegal activities of the FBI and COINTELPRO.

COINTELPRO—DIVIDE AND DISRUPT

By 1968, COINTELPRO targeted many protest groups. COINTELPRO burglars stole money, files, and equipment. Government spies tried to turn blacks and whites against each other. They spread false rumors about leaders. They also tried to turn workers and students against each other.

COINTELPRO spied on protesters, tapped their telephones, and opened their mail. FBI agents made anonymous phone calls and sent phony letters to people. They arrested people on false charges. Agents joined activist groups in order to spy on them.

Sometimes the FBI framed people. They provided **phony** evidence to police. Some people went to jail on false charges. They were victims of COINTELPRO.

In 1971, secret COINTELPRO files were taken from FBI offices and given to the press. When the public found out what the FBI had done, this secret program was stopped.

TWO WARS

By 1968, the United States was fighting two wars. First, the government had sent soldiers to fight in Vietnam. Second, the government had sent the FBI and COINTELPRO to fight protesters at home.

Antiwar protesters

5

CHAPTER

Running for President

For some Americans, 1968 offered a last chance to change the country for the better. Maybe they could make **system** work after all. Maybe they could elect a good president. Maybe they could change society through politics.

One journalist remembered the spring of 1968 as a "rare moment." She said it was "a happy time in American politics. You felt you could do something."

LBJ was president, and he planned to run again. Would the Democratic Party support him? Most people thought it would. He was a Democratic president. His own party would never abandon him.

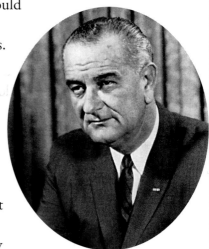

President Lyndon B. Johnson

"CLEAN FOR GENE"

Democratic Senator Eugene McCarthy disagreed. He opposed the Vietnam War. He felt most Democrats would agree with him. He decided to run against Johnson.

34

Senator Eugene McCarthy

McCarthy represented Minnesota in the United States Senate. He held **liberal** values. He supported civil rights and the War on Poverty. But he opposed the war in Vietnam.

Hubert Humphrey had been a senator from Minnesota. He and McCarthy had been close allies. Now Humphrey was LBJ's vice president. Now Humphrey and McCarthy found themselves on opposing sides.

On November 30, 1967, McCarthy made his stand. He announced that he would run for president. His reason for running was his opposition to the war.

Across the country, young people rushed to support him. Hundreds left colleges to work on his **campaign**. Some left their jobs. These volunteers slept on gym floors. They knocked on doors and handed out **leaflets**.

McCarthy supporters knew many voters disliked "hippies." So the workers went "clean for Gene." Many cut their hair and shaved their beards. They began wearing **conservative** clothing. They wanted people to pay attention to their message, not their hair or clothes.

Hippies were young people of the 1960s and 1970s. The hippie movement spread from the United States to Canada, England, and several other countries.

Hippies protested society's customs and traditions. Most hippies were 17 to 25 years old and from white middle-class families. In 1967, about 300,000 young people left home to join the movement.

Hippies believed in love and peace. They felt people should say what they thought and act naturally. They were against the Vietnam War, wealth, and discrimination against all minorities. Hippies were often called flower children because they used flowers as a symbol of love.

Hippies lived together in small groups and shared one another's belongings. They wore strange-looking clothes, grew their hair long, and wore sandals or went barefoot. Many used drugs.

In time, most hippies realized they could not reform society by "dropping out" of it. So many fought for political and social change in more conventional ways.

In the United States election system, primary elections are held first. In a primary election, Democrats choose one candidate from all Democratics running for a particular office. Republicans choose from among Republican candidates. This time, Democrats had to choose between Eugene McCarthy and President Johnson.

Some of McCarthy's supporters felt frustrated. They thought he spoke too quietly. They wanted more fire and enthusiasm. No one doubted his intelligence or **integrity**. They just wanted him to shout and pound the table. But that was not his style.

New Hampshire held the first primary on March 12. No one thought McCarthy could win. But **optimists** said he might get 28 percent of the vote. Others laughed at that number.

When the polls closed, McCarthy had won 42.4 percent of the vote. Johnson received 49.5 percent.

The experts were amazed. No one thought McCarthy would do so well. This was a great victory! The *Boston Globe* headline read, "McCarthy's N.H. Dream Becomes LBJ Nightmare."

In five months, Democrats planned to meet in Chicago. The Democratic National Convention would choose a presidential candidate. McCarthy's campaign continued.

ANOTHER KENNEDY CAMPAIGNS

John Kennedy had been assassinated in 1963. His younger brother, Robert Kennedy, had been his **attorney general**. Bobby Kennedy and LBJ disliked each other, so Bobby Kennedy gave up the attorney general job when LBJ became president.

Bobby Kennedy decided to run for the Senate. By 1968, he was Senator Robert Kennedy of New York.

Many wanted Bobby Kennedy to run for president. They thought he would make a good president. They had loved JFK. Now they wanted Bobby to take his place.

At first, Bobby Kennedy did not agree. He thought no Democrat could beat LBJ. After New Hampshire, he changed his mind.

Senator Robert Kennedy announces his candidacy.

A few days after the primary, Bobby Kennedy agreed to run. McCarthy was angry. His supporters were furious.

McCarthy's people thought Kennedy would split the peace vote. He would split the party and hand the nomination to LBJ.

McCarthy supporters felt that McCarthy had announced that he would run first. He risked challenging LBJ, so he deserved the nomination. Kennedy should support McCarthy.

But Kennedy entered the race anyway. His campaign took off quickly. He spoke **eloquently**. His young, handsome, and enthusiastic looks attracted many supporters.

THE FINAL MARCH SURPRISE

March was a great month. McCarthy made a great showing in New Hampshire. Bobby Kennedy launched a campaign. And the month had not yet ended. But the nation was in for another surprise.

On March 31, 1968, President Lyndon Johnson sat before television cameras. He announced that he would not run for reelection.

> With America's sons in the fields far away, with America's future under challenge right here at home, with our hopes and the world's hopes for peace in the balance every day, I do not believe that I should devote an hour or a day of my time to any personal **partisan** causes or to any duties other than the awesome duties of this office—the presidency of your country.
>
> Accordingly, I shall not seek, and I will not accept, the nomination of my party for another term as your president.

The nation was stunned. The news hit front pages on April Fool's Day, but it was no joke.

Years later, Johnson explained his decision.

> I felt that I was being chased on all sides by a giant **stampede**. I was being forced over the edge by rioting blacks, demonstrating students, marching welfare mothers, squawking professors, and hysterical supporters.

Worst of all, Johnson said, was Bobby. Bobby Kennedy was coming "to reclaim the throne in the memory of his brother. And the American people, swayed by the magic of the name, were dancing in the streets."

LBJ would not run again, but McCarthy and Kennedy were still in the race. Soon, a new candidate joined them.

THE NEW CANDIDATE

Vice President Hubert Humphrey joined the campaign. Humphrey did not like the Vietnam War. But as vice president, he could not speak against it. He could not oppose the policies of LBJ. He had to support the record of the administration.

BLOODY SPRING

Four days after LBJ's announcement, Dr. Martin Luther King was killed. Cities erupted in riots, smoke, and gunfire. Many thought the country had lost its last and best hope for unity.

As the smoke cleared, the presidential campaign continued. Now it seemed grim. Could anyone make a difference? Or was this nation too far sunk in violence to change?

BLOODY CAMPUS

In late April 1968, the spotlight shifted. Students at Columbia University **rebelled**. They sat in the buildings on campus and refused to go to classes.

In part, their protest focused on community issues. The university sat next to a black community. The university planned to build a new gym. The community opposed the gym, but the university did not care. The students supported the community.

The gym was only part of the reason for the protest. Students wanted more power within the university.

Mark Rudd was a student leader. Grayson Kirk was president of Columbia University. Rudd wrote to Kirk.

> Grayson, I doubt if you will understand any of this.…
> you call for order and respect for authority; we call
> for justice, freedom, and **socialism**.

Columbia's president refused to give an inch.

On April 30, police invaded campus. They hauled out all the protesters, injuring many. They arrested more than 700 students. A month later, it all happened again.

Hope was disappearing fast.

CALIFORNIA

Yet, McCarthy and Kennedy supporters clung to hope. Through April and May, the two men campaigned across the nation. In June, they clashed in California.

The California primary was important. The winner would be the clear front-runner. He would probably win the nomination in August. Kennedy and McCarthy both campaigned hard.

Kennedy won big. He celebrated at the Ambassador Hotel. First, he stayed with friends in his **suite**. They watched news reports. But a crowd of supporters waited downstairs. They wanted Bobby to speak to them.

After midnight, Kennedy went downstairs and spoke to the crowd. He thanked everyone. He called for McCarthy's supporters to join him.

> Not for myself, but for the cause and the ideas
> which moved you to begin this great popular
> movement.

> What I think … is that we can work together. We are
> a great country, an unselfish country, and a
> compassionate country.

The crowd cheered wildly.

Kennedy turned to leave through the hotel kitchen. He stopped to shake hands with a dishwasher. Then he fell to the floor. He had been shot. Five other people were wounded.

His companions seized the killer. Sirhan Sirhan was a 24-year-old man with a $31-dollar gun.

Sirhan Sirhan, a Palestinian Arab, was captured at the scene. He was later tried, convicted of murder, and sentenced to death. Before the sentence could be carried out, the United States Supreme Court declared the death penalty unconstitutional. Sirhan is currently serving a life sentence in Corcoran State Prison in California.

Ted Kennedy, the only surviving Kennedy brother, spoke at Bobby Kennedy's funeral. He asked people to remember Bobby, "simply as a good and decent man, who saw wrong and tried to right it, saw suffering and tried to heal it, saw war and tried to stop it."

The nation reeled in shock. Yet another leader had been assassinated.

A popular song mourned that the good die young. In his song "Abraham, Martin, and John," Dion Demucil asked people to love and remember the things these three men stood for. He wrote that Bobby was now in the company of Abraham Lincoln, Dr. Martin Luther King, and his brother, John.

6
CHAPTER

Hippies and Yippies

Not everyone looked to politics for answers. Many young people dropped out. They dropped out of school and jobs. They dropped out of "regular" life.

HIPPIES

What was a hippie? Sandals and love beads. Drugs and rock and roll. Long hair and blue jeans. Each of us has an image of hippies.

If the images are different, that's okay. Hippies were different too. Some took lots of drugs. Others took none. Some wore lots of beads. Others did not.

Hippies wanted a different world. They wanted a world built on love. Love was more important than politics. They believed love was more important than even money. They valued music and beauty. They wanted freedom to express themselves. They wanted love and freedom for everyone.

An older hippie

Sometimes hippies lived in **communes**. They shared incomes and expenses. They even shared childcare duties. Some communes were on farms. Some were in cities. Some hippies worked, and some did not.

Some hippies were also activists. They worked for social change. They worked for civil rights or protested the war.

Hippies were nonviolent. Many marched on the Pentagon in a demonstration against the Vietnam War. Soldiers with guns stood guard. The hippies put flowers in their gun barrels.

Other hippies disliked politics. They just wanted to live in peace. They refused to protest.

SUMMERS OF LOVE

The first summer of love came in 1966. It happened in San Francisco. Many artists and musicians lived there. Hippies traveled to San Francisco from all over the country. Many hung out on beaches. Others stayed in Golden Gate Park and experimented with drugs. Free music floated through the air.

Scott McKenzie wrote a song, "San Francisco," about that summer of 1967 and urged people to come to San Francisco and wear flowers in their hair.

"The flowers felt right," he said, "because everyone we knew was trying to save the world peacefully with flowers as symbols." McKenzie's song promised that summertime in San Francisco would be a "love-in."

Abbie Hoffman is stopped by the police.

THE YIPPIES

Abbie Hoffman was a hippie fighting for social change. He worked for civil rights in the early sixties. Then his focus changed.

In the beginning, he saw a system that oppressed black Americans. Then he saw that the system oppressed others too. Abbie Hoffman rebelled against the **establishment**. And he did it with style.

In 1967, Hoffman went to New York. He wanted to protest against greed. He created a protest that looked like a theater performance.

Hoffman gathered a few friends. They went to the New York Stock Exchange. They climbed the stairs to an upper balcony. Once there, they threw money onto the floor below. They scattered one- and five-dollar bills.

The stockbrokers suddenly stopped trading. Men in suits grabbed for the falling bills. There was almost a riot as greed overtook the traders.

Guards threw out the demonstrators. Hoffman and his friends danced in the street. Then they burned the remaining money. Their actions got lots of attention. This, thought Hoffman, was a great way to protest!

Hoffman believed that protest was part of citizenship. "Democracy," Hoffman often said, "is not a spectator sport."

Hoffman and Jerry Rubin formed a new protest group. They called it the Youth International Party, or Yippies.

ON TO CHICAGO

By late summer of 1968, the country's focus had shifted. San Francisco was not the happening place. All eyes were on Chicago.

The Democrats were going to Chicago. They would choose a candidate for president. The Yippies were ready. They would go to Chicago too. They planned to stage the "Festival of Life." It would be the protest of the year.

7

Chicago

June, July, August. McCarthy's campaign marched on. He would go to Chicago, but he did not have enough votes for the nomination. Bobby Kennedy was dead. So the Democrats would probably choose Humphrey.

But activists refused to give up. They could not let Humphrey have the nomination without protest.

YIPPIE THEATER

The Yippies organized a theater-type demonstration for Chicago. The protesters planned to live in a Chicago park. They would bring "free food, tents, theater, underground newspapers and lots of rock bands and singers."

Other protest groups made wild suggestions too. Many of their proposals seemed made for headlines. They talked about adding drugs to Chicago's water supply. Some promised to float nude in Lake Michigan.

The Yippies bought a pig and named it Pigasus. They planned to nominate Pigasus for president. The Yippies invited everyone to join them.

The Yippies wanted to camp in Grant Park. They applied for permits. The city said no. The Yippies came anyway.

PROTEST PLANS

Other activists had plans too. The MOBE planned to march in the streets. MOBE was the National Mobilization to End the War in Vietnam. Many groups belonged to the MOBE. They planned to join in the demonstration against the war.

David Dellinger explained their position.

> Whoever the candidates are and whatever the platforms, . . . we must stay in the streets and stay in active **resistance** or else there will be no peace. Either in the ghettos or in Vietnam.

MOBE did not oppose the Yippies. They just had different plans for protest.

MOBE wanted to march in the streets. They applied for permits to march. The city said no. The MOBE came anyway. So did Vets for Peace, the Black Panthers, and the Students for a Democratic Society (SDS).

LINCOLN PARK: THE BEGINNING

Richard J. Daley was mayor of Chicago. He didn't like the activists, and he didn't want any demonstrations in his quiet, orderly city. He wanted a peaceful convention, and he wanted Hubert Humphrey to get the nomination.

Chicago police sent spies to the protests. So did the FBI and COINTELPRO. The spies joined the demonstrators and reported on their plans.

The first night, protesters gathered in Lincoln Park. Police attacked. Some protesters fought back, swore at police, or threw rocks. Most remained peaceful.

The police had weapons and **tear gas**. They used both. The night air filled with tear gas. It caused tears and burning eyes, noses, and throats.

Nearby residents closed their windows. They coughed and choked inside their apartments.

Chaos reigned outside. Police chased people down the sidewalks. They arrested anyone they caught. Those under 18 were charged with curfew violation. Others were charged with disorderly conduct or resisting arrest. Police beat many people instead of arresting them.

Reporters roamed Lincoln Park taking photos of the police in action. So the police attacked the reporters too. Still, stories of police violence made the news.

GRANT PARK

The second night in Lincoln Park was less violent. Attention had shifted to Grant Park.

Grant Park was in downtown Chicago, closer to the Convention Center. The park was across the street from the Hilton Hotel where many **delegates** were staying.

Thousands of demonstrators gathered. One teen tried to remove an American flag from a pole. Police arrested him. Other activists took down the flag.

Fury filled the police. They would not allow demonstrators to disrespect the flag! Police attacked the demonstrators, using tear gas, **Mace**, and clubs.

Most demonstrators were nonviolent, but a few fought back. They threw eggs, bricks, and stones.

Angry police attacked bystanders, convention delegates, and reporters. It seemed they attacked anyone who was not in uniform. News reports called it a police riot.

Police arrest a protester in Grant Park.

Armed guards surround Grant Park.

Outside the convention, a reporter talked to a protest leader.

"Do you have a permit to march?" he asked.

"No," the leader answered. "There were no permits to march."

"But you're going to march anyway? Do you expect trouble?"

"Yes," the leader said. "We expect to march. We expect trouble all the time."

THE WHOLE WORLD IS WATCHING

Mary Turck, the author, was a college student in Chicago. She and her friends, Val and Mirian, worked for civil rights and opposed the war. At first, they did not plan to demonstrate.

Then the young women saw the violence on television. They saw police beating young people and decided they had to take sides. They went downtown to join the demonstration.

Michigan Avenue is a wide, beautiful street. On its east side, trees and rose gardens grow in Grant Park. Fashionable shops and hotels line the west side. Downtown streets bustle with traffic. Chicago is a busy, lively city.

On that August day, downtown Chicago seemed deserted. The streets were almost empty. Instead of business traffic, tanks blocked Michigan Avenue.

Police carried shields and guns. Medics moved freely on the streets. They wore Red Cross armbands. But they weren't sure the armbands would protect them from the police.

The whole scene seemed unreal to the three students. Their city had tanks in the streets. Their city, with medics walking around, looked like a war zone. Chicago police officers were now the enemy.

The three young women joined the demonstrators in Grant Park. They sang, "Give Peace a Chance." They chanted, "The streets belong to the people."

The afternoon wore on. Rumors ran through the crowd. The police were coming. No, they were just forming a line along the sidewalk. They were pulling back. No, they had surrounded the park. They wanted to arrest everyone.

Suddenly, the gas came. People ran, stumbled, and fell. Val could not see. Mirian could not stand up alone. Holding on to one another, the trio tried to leave. But there was no place to go.

Eventually, they escaped. That night at home, they watched television coverage. Their eyes still stung from the tear gas. On television, they saw police beating demonstrators. They heard the crowd chant, "The whole world is watching!"

The army sent a military intelligence unit. The unit filmed the demonstrations each day. Then the film was flown to the FBI in Washington, D.C., each night.

How many demonstrators came to Chicago? No one knows for sure. The best estimate says more than 10,000 demonstrated. About half of these came from out of town. The rest were Chicagoans. More than 1,000 were probably police and federal spies.

INSIDE THE CONVENTION

Inside the convention center, tension grew. A security agent punched TV reporter Dan Rather. He was just one of the reporters on the scene and the police and security agents were furious with the press.

Other reporters also became targets. Dozens were hit or punched during the week. Many were arrested.

Delegates split into hostile camps. Some proposed adding a peace **plank** to the **platform**. This would be an official statement in favor of peace. The vote was 1567 to 1041. Peace lost.

Some delegates put on black armbands. The armbands were symbols of opposition. Others sang "We Shall Overcome." The mood grew more bitter.

Many delegates opposed the war. They supported civil rights. They agreed with the protesters. They were outraged by the Chicago police. More than 500 delegates marched with candles in a funeral march for peace.

Finally, the convention delegates chose Hubert Humphrey to run for president. The convention ended, but the violence did not.

Early the next morning after the convention ended, police dragged some of McCarthy's campaign workers from their hotel rooms. They had been dropping things from the windows on the fifteenth floor.

The police beat the workers. Then they took them to the hotel lobby.

Finally, someone woke McCarthy. He came down and rescued his workers.

CHAPTER

The Election

The conventions were over. The campaign was not nearly as exciting.

UNHAPPY WARRIOR

Hubert Humphrey was a liberal. He supported civil rights. He had spoken out for civil rights as early as 1948. He also supported the War on Poverty and equal education.

Before becoming vice president, Humphrey had been a senator from Minnesota. He gave great speeches and enjoyed meeting people. He loved politics. People called him the "Happy Warrior."

In 1964, LBJ had asked him to run for vice president. The Vietnam War was not a major issue yet. Humphrey and LBJ had agreed on civil rights, helping poor people, and improving public education. Humphrey accepted the vice-presidency.

Hubert Humphrey

By 1968, Humphrey was no longer a Happy Warrior. He did not like the Vietnam War. But as vice president, he could not speak out against the war. He felt he had to support LBJ's policies.

Americans forgot that Humphrey supported civil rights. Now he was known for making war on Vietnam.

Many of Humphrey's old friends hated the war. They had turned against Humphrey and worked for Kennedy or McCarthy. They didn't support Humphrey any longer.

ONE MORE TIME

Richard Nixon had served as vice president in the 1950s under President Dwight Eisenhower. He ran for president against John F. Kennedy in 1960 and lost.

Nixon ran for governor of California. He lost that race also. He became bitter. For a while, he dropped out of politics.

In 1968, Richard Nixon came back. The Republicans nominated him for president. He agreed to run one more time.

Nixon was a conservative. He hated the protesters. He had never supported civil rights. He thought the War on Poverty was wasteful.

Richard Nixon campaigns for the presidency.

Nixon feared Communists wanted to take over the country. He thought they were protest leaders.

He promised "law and order" at home. That meant getting tough on protest and on crime. He promised "peace with honor" in Vietnam. That meant winning the war.

Nixon ran with Spiro Agnew. Agnew claimed Humphrey was "squishy soft on Communism." And he said "If you've seen one **slum**, you've seen them all."

THE WALLACE FACTOR

A strong third-party candidate entered the presidential race. George Wallace was Alabama's governor. He resisted **integration**. "**Segregation** now," he declared. "Segregation tomorrow. Segregation forever!"

His appeal was strong in the South where many Americans held racist views.

PROTEST ON THE CAMPAIGN TRAIL

Protesters followed Humphrey everywhere. Some called him foul names. They spit on him and his wife. They called her names too.

Humphrey grew angry with them. Years later, he talked about the campaign.

> How do you think you would like that, day after day, month after month? By people who say they believe in peace and brotherly love? I just couldn't quite take that. After a while I got to looking at these people and saying, "Well, they're just not decent people."

The protesters did not attack Nixon. They knew what he stood for, and they didn't agree. But with Humphrey it was different. Once he had been a friend, but now they felt he had betrayed them.

Near the end of the campaign, Humphrey spoke for peace. He proposed an end to bombing North Vietnam. At the last minute, McCarthy **endorsed** Humphrey. Kennedy supporters came to his side too. Protests wound down. One sign at a rally said, "If you mean it, we're with you."

At the end of October, LBJ stopped the bombing. The North Vietnamese agreed to peace talks. Then the South Vietnamese backed away. They refused the peace talks. The South Vietnamese thought they could get a better deal from Nixon. They would not talk about peace until after the election.

So the war continued.

NIXON WINS

The moves toward peace were too little, too late for Humphrey. Nixon won the 1968 election with 31,170,470 **popular votes**. He received 301 **electoral college votes**.

Humphrey came close. He won 30,898,055 popular votes. But he received only 191 electoral votes.

Wallace received 9,906,473 popular votes and 46 electoral votes.

CHAPTER 9

The Darkest Days

Richard Nixon became president in January of 1969. The Vietnam War ground on.

DEATH IN VIETNAM

More than 500,000 United States soldiers were in Vietnam. About 200 United States soldiers were killed each week. Another 800 were wounded. Almost 500 South Vietnamese soldiers died weekly.

Despite these losses, the south seemed to be winning. Every day, they counted more than 500 Viet Cong and North Vietnamese dead.

In July, President Nixon announced a new policy. He called it Vietnamization. He said United States ground troops would come home. They would leave the South Vietnamese army to fight its own war. The United States would give the South Vietnamese weapons and equipment. The United States would continue bombing North Vietnam.

Soldiers began to come home. In Vietnam, the killing continued. United States and South Vietnamese troops invaded Cambodia.

United States Senator Birch Bayh spoke for many Americans. "I cannot believe," he said, "that a plan for peace necessitates bombing four countries, invading two, in order to get out of one."

Peace talks continued, sometimes in public and sometimes in secret. The Vietnam War would drag on until 1973.

A peace agreement was reached and signed on January 27, 1973, by the United States, North Vietnam, South Vietnam, and the National Liberation Front (Viet Cong). This agreement provided for the end of the war, the withdrawal of the United States troops, the return of prisoners of war, and the formation of a four-nation international control commission to ensure peace.

Fighting continued between North and South Vietnam until early 1975 when the North Vietnamese marched into Saigon. Vietnam was formally reunified in July 1976.

DEATH AT HOME

Protests continued across the United States. At Kent State University in Ohio, the National Guard fired on protesters. They killed four students and wounded nine more. At Jackson State in Mississippi, police fired on black students. They killed two students and wounded ten. They left dormitories marked with 200 bullet holes.

President Nixon drew up an "enemies list." He ordered government officials to spy on these enemies. Protesters, civil rights leaders, and other politicians headed the list.

CHICAGO SEVEN

In 1968, before the Democratic Convention, Congress had passed an antiriot act. Eight leaders of the Chicago protests were charged under that act. They went on trial in 1969.

(from left to right) William Kunstler (lawyer), Abbie Hoffman, Dave Dellinger, Jerry Rubin, and Gerry Lefcort (lawyer) surrender to federal arrest in New York City.

Black Panther Bobby Seale was one of the eight leaders charged. When Seale's lawyer was hospitalized, Seale demanded the right to represent himself. The judge refused. Bobby Seale protested loudly in court. The judge ordered him bound and gagged. Then the judge ordered Seale held for a separate trial.

And he also sentenced Seale to four years in jail for **contempt**. The Chicago Eight were now the Chicago Seven.

The trial was held in Chicago before Judge Julius Hoffman. Some of the defendants wanted to be serious. Abbie Hoffman (no relation to the judge) did not. As the trial proceeded, it seemed more like a theater than a courtroom.

Abbie Hoffman testified in the trial. His testimony continued his protest. Hoffman was questioned by defense lawyer Leonard Weinglass.

> **MR. WEINGLASS:** When were you born?
>
> **HOFFMAN:** Psychologically, 1960. . . .
>
> **MR. WEINGLASS:** What is the actual date of your birth?
>
> **HOFFMAN:** November 30, 1936.
>
> **MR. WEINGLASS:** Between the date of your birth, November 30, 1936, and May 1, 1960, what, if anything, occurred in your life?
>
> **HOFFMAN:** Nothing. I believe it is called an American education. . . .
>
> **MR. WEINGLASS:** Can you tell the Court and jury what is your present occupation?
>
> **HOFFMAN:** I am a cultural revolutionary. Well, I am really a defendant—full-time.
>
> **MR. WEINGLASS:** What do you mean by the phrase *cultural revolutionary*?
>
> **HOFFMAN:** Well, I suppose it is a person who tries to shape and participate in the values and the **mores**, the customs and the style of living of new people who eventually become inhabitants of a new nation and a new society through art and poetry, theater, and music.

Throughout the trial, Judge Julius Hoffman showed his dislike of the defendants—and of their lawyers. His rulings favored the government attorneys.

Finally, the trial ended. The jury found David Dellinger, Abbie Hoffman, Jerry Rubin, Tom Hayden, and Rennie Davis guilty. John Froines and Lee Weiner were found not guilty.

Judge Julius Hoffman sentenced all five. Then he sentenced them again for contempt of court.

Judge Hoffman found the defense attorneys guilty too. He sentenced defense attorneys Leonard Weinglass and William Kunstler for contempt of court.

All the defendants—and their attorneys—appealed. The appeals court threw out their convictions.

SURVIVING THE SIXTIES

The Black Panther Party died in the 1970s. Some of its members still found their way into the news. Former Panther Bobby Seale ran for mayor of Oakland, California, in 1973. He didn't win, but he did receive about 40% of the vote. In Chicago, former Panther Bobby Rush was elected to Congress in 1992.

Tom Hayden, another protest leader, was elected to the California legislature. He served there for 16 years.

Despite the war and despite the killings, hope never quite died. People continued to work for a better world, love their country, and to protest injustice.

New dreams—and new dreamers—are born every year.

SOURCES

Eisele, Albert. *Almost to the Presidency: A Biography of Two American Politicians*, Piper Company, Blue Earth, MN, 1972.

Kaiser, Charles. *1968 in America: Music, Politics, Chaos, Counterculture and the Shaping of a Generation*, Grove Press, New York, 1997.

Kearns, Doris. *Lyndon Johnson and the American Dream*, Harper, New York, NY, 1976.

WBGH. American Experience: Vietnam The WGBH Educational Foundation produced a 13-part television retrospective, *Vietnam: A Television History*. It was broadcast by the Public Broadcasting Service starting in October 1983.

Zinn, Howard. *A People's History of the United States: 1492–Present*, HarperPerennial, New York, NY, 1996.

GLOSSARY

activist	person who strongly supports or opposes an issue
assassination	murder or killing by a swift attack
attorney general	chief law officer of a nation who advises and represents the government in legal matters
brutality	harsh or severe action against another person
campaign	connected series of events used to bring about a particular result such as an election
chaos	state of utter confusion
civil rights	the personal freedoms that are guaranteed to United States citizens by the Constitution and by acts of Congress
commitment	promise to do something
commune	group of people who live together and share everything
Communist	one who believes in a government that owns all business and industry
comrade	companion or friend
conservative	one who believes in traditional methods or views
contempt	lack of respect for something
corrupt	having changed from good to bad
counterintelligence	organized activity designed to gather political and military information, to prevent sabotage, and to confuse the enemy

court-martial	to bring a member of the armed forces to a trial held before military officers
curfew	specified time after which people are forbidden to be out on the streets
czar	title given the ruler of Russia until 1917
declaration	announcement
deferment	official delay of serving in the military
delegate	appointed representative
depression	period of low economic activity marked by rising levels of unemployment
desert	to leave military duty without permission with no plans to return
dictator	one who has complete control of a government
discrimination	act of treating someone differently because he or she belongs to a minority group
disrespect	lack of consideration or respect
draft	act of selecting an individual for military service
electoral college vote	body that elects the president and vice president of the United States. Each state has the same number of electors as it has senators and representatives. Each member of the electoral college casts one vote for the candidate that received the most popular votes during the national election in his or her home state.
eloquently	with forceful and vivid expression
endorse	to support
establishment	common group of society that includes the social, economic, and political leaders

fit	being physically and mentally suitable to do something
flank	right or left side
foreign	having to do with a country other than one's own
gallantry	great bravery
ghetto	section of a city in which members of a minority group live especially because of social, legal, or economic pressures
glitz	excessive showiness
grieving	having great sorrow, pain, or suffering
guerrilla	having irregular war practices such as harassment or sabotage
inaugural	relating to the ceremony in which a president is sworn into office
integration	act of giving all citizens equal opportunities regardless of race, religion, or sex
integrity	quality of following a set of morals and values
just	being legal, fair, and necessary
leaflet	folded printed sheet designed as a free handout
liberal	one who is open-minded and willing to listen to opinions that are not necessarily those that are accepted by the majority of people
Mace	strong liquid chemical spray that is used to disable a person
march	organized procession of demonstrators who are supporting or protesting something

mores	fixed customs of a particular group
National Guard	state military unit funded equally by the federal and state governments
negotiate	to talk with one another so as to arrive at a settlement of differences
optimist	person who sees the favorable side of everything
parallel	one of the lines of latitude that circles the earth
partisan	strictly following policies of one party, cause, or person
patriot	one who loves and supports his or her country
peaceful resistance	act of protesting or demonstrating without the use of force or violence
petition	formal written request
phony	fake
plank	issue on the platform (see separate glossary entry) of a political party
platform	list of policies adopted by a political party or candidate
popular vote	relating to the votes of the general public
progressive	believing in government of moderate political change and social improvement
racism	belief that one race is superior to all others
rebel	to oppose or go against
refuge	place that provides shelter or protection
resistance	act of opposing
retarded	to show a delay in normal academic progress

reunite	to bring back together
row house	one of a series of houses connected by common sidewalls to form a continuous group
segregation	act of being separated by class, race, religion, or sex
slum	densely populated urban area having crowded, dirty, run-down housing
socialism	belief that the production and distribution of goods should be controlled by the government. The distribution of goods and pay depends on work done.
stampede	act of being overwhelmed by the demands of others
strike	to stop work in order to force employers to agree to employees' demands
subside	to quiet down or become less
suite	group of rooms in a single unit
system	social, economic, or political organization
tear gas	solid, liquid, or gas that when released blinds the eyes with tears
treaty	agreement to end an armed conflict between countries
tutor	private teacher
union	group of workers who join together and work for better conditions
veteran	person who has served in one of the armed forces
vigil	act of evening prayer and devotion

INDEX

Agnew, Spiro, 57

American flag, 26–27, 29, 51

Banks, Captain Edward, 17

Bayh, Birch, 61

Berrigan, Daniel, 26

Berrigan, Philip, 25–26

Black Panther Party for
Self-Defense, 30, 31–32, 50,
62, 64

Cabrini Green, 6–8, 11

Carmichael, Stokely, 22

Chicago, Illinois, 6, 11, 32, 37,
47, 48–54, 62, 63, 64

Chicago Seven, 62–64

civil rights, 5, 9–10, 11, 18, 19,
28, 30, 35, 45, 46, 54, 55, 56

COINTELPRO, 30, 32, 33, 50

Columbia University, 40–41

Commission on Civil Disorders
(Kerner Commission), 8–9

Communists, 13, 14, 18, 28,
30, 57

conscientious objectors (COs),
20–21

Daley, Richard J., 50

Davis, Rennie, 64

Dellinger, David, 49, 62, 64

Democratic Convention, 37, 47,
54, 62

draft, 20–23, 25, 26

Eisenhower, Dwight, 15, 56

Fallows, James, 20–21

Federal Bureau of Investigation
(FBI), 26, 30–33, 50, 53

France, 13, 14, 15

Freedom of Information Act, 32

Froines, John, 64

Hampton, Fred, 32

Harris, David, 23

Hayden, Tom, 64

hippies, 35–36, 43, 44–45

Ho Chi Minh, 14, 15, 18

Hoffman, Abbie, 46–47, 62, 63,
64

Hoffman, Julius, 63, 64

Hoover, J. Edgar, 30

Humphrey, Hubert, 35, 40, 48,
50, 54, 55–56, 57–58

Jackson State University, 61

Johnson, Lyndon Baines (LBJ), 5,
8, 16, 18, 22, 34, 35, 37, 38,
39, 40, 55, 56, 58

Kennedy, John F. (JFK), 4–5, 16,
37, 56

Kennedy, Robert, 37–40, 41–42, 48, 56, 58

Kennedy, Ted, 42

Kent State University, 61

Kerner, Otto, 8

King Jr., Dr. Martin Luther, 9–11, 19, 22, 30, 31, 40

Kirk, Grayson, 41

Kunstler, William, 62, 64

McCarthy, Eugene, 34–35, 37, 38, 39, 40, 41, 48, 54, 56, 58

Memphis, Tennessee, 9

National Association for the Advancement of Colored People (NAACP), 22

National Liberation Front (Viet Cong), 16, 17, 60, 61

National Mobilization to End the War in Vietnam (MOBE), 49–50

Newton, Huey P., 31

New York Stock Exchange, 46–47

Ngo Dinh Diem, 14–15, 16

Nixon, Richard, 56–58, 59, 60, 61

North Vietnamese Army (NVA), 16, 17

Oswald, Lee Harvey, 5

pacifists, 18, 21

Peace Corps, 5

Rather, Dan, 54

Ray, James Earl, 10

Ruby, Jack, 5

Rubin, Jerry, 47, 62, 64

Rudd, Mark, 41

Rush, Bobby, 64

Russia, 14

Seale, Bobby, 31, 62–63, 64

Sirhan Sirhan, 42

Smith, Mike, 26–27

Stennis, John, 30

Student Nonviolent Coordinating Committee (SNCC), 22

Students for a Democratic Society (SDS), 50

Vets for Peace, 50

Viet Minh, 13, 14, 15

Vietnam, 12, 13–17, 18, 22, 23, 26, 28, 29, 33, 35, 49, 57, 58, 59, 60, 61

Vietnam Veterans Against the War, 24

Vietnam War, 15–18, 19, 21, 23–24, 25, 26, 27, 28, 29, 30, 33, 34, 35, 36, 40, 45, 49, 55, 56, 57, 59–61

Wallace, George, 57, 58

War on Poverty, 5, 28, 35, 55, 56

Warner, Ivan, 27

Weiner, Lee, 64

Weinglass, Leonard, 63, 64

Wilkins, Roy, 22

Youth International Party (Yippies), 47, 48, 50